J. S. Bach: 50 Solos

FOR CLASSICAL GUITAR

Arranged by Mark Phillips

To access audio visit:
www.halleonard.com/mylibrary

4685-2145-2490-4672

Cherry Lane Music Company
Director of Publications/Project Editor: Mark Phillips
Publications Coordinator: Gabrielle Fastman

ISBN 978-1-57560-885-3

Visit Hal Leonard Online at
www.halleonard.com

Aria - Cantata No. 1

Johann Sebastian Bach

Moderately

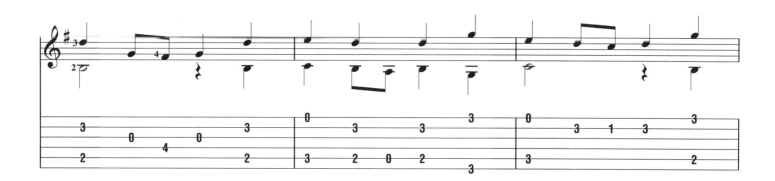

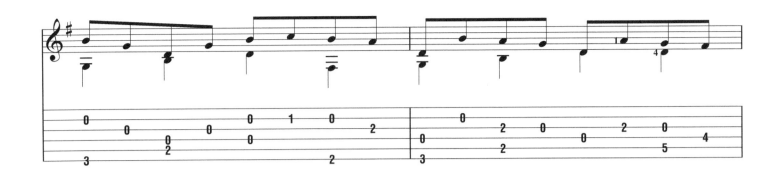

Aria - Cantata No. 2

TRACK 2

Johann Sebastian Bach

Moderately slow, in 2

Aria - Cantata No. 3

Johann Sebastian Bach

TRACK 3

Slowly, in 2

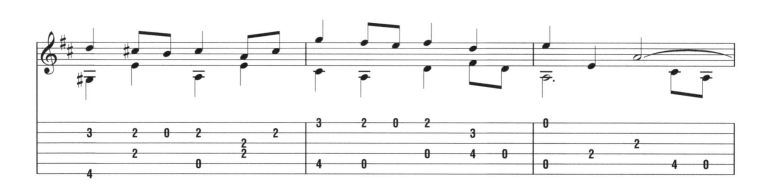

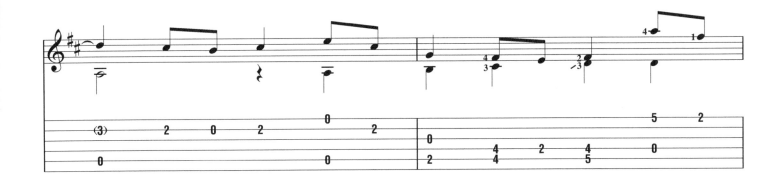

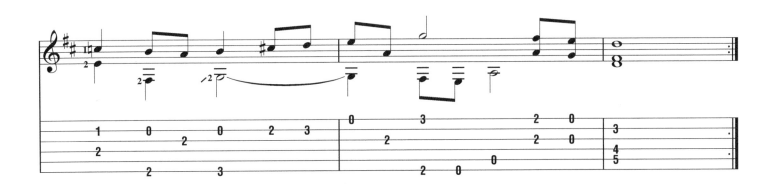

Aria - Cantata No. 6

TRACK 4

Johann Sebastian Bach

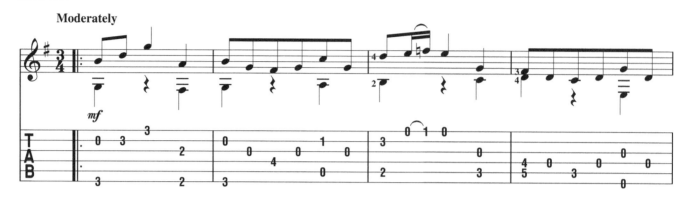

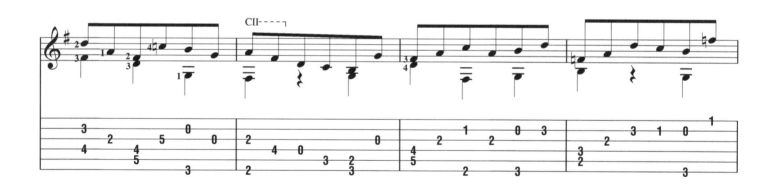

Aria - Cantata No. 36

TRACK 5

Johann Sebastian Bach

Moderately

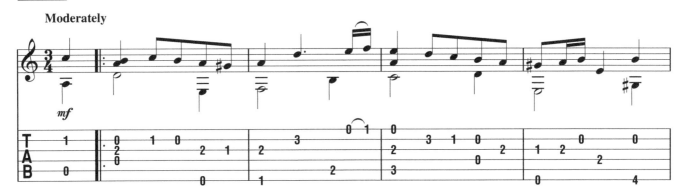

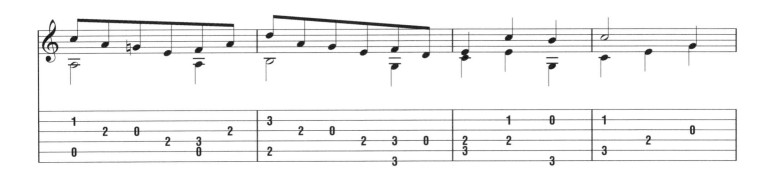

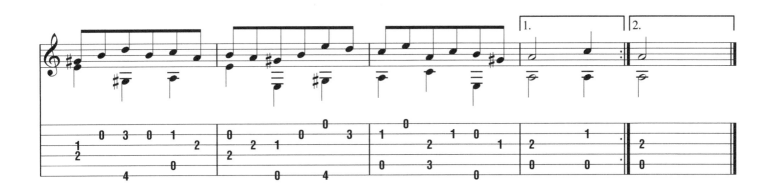

Aria - Cantata No. 21

TRACK 6

Johann Sebastian Bach

Moderately slow, in 2

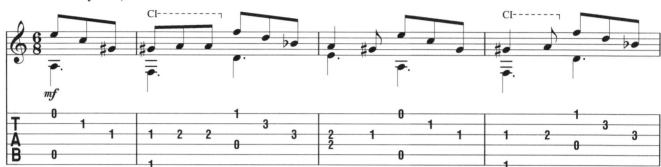

Aria - Cantata No. 22

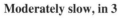

Johann Sebastian Bach

Moderately slow, in 3

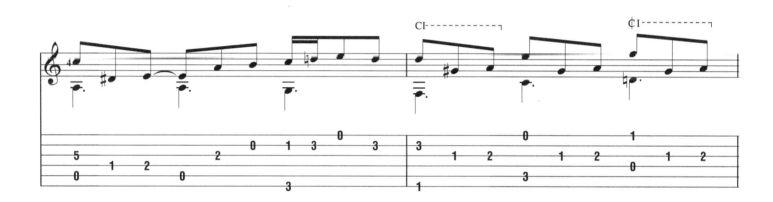

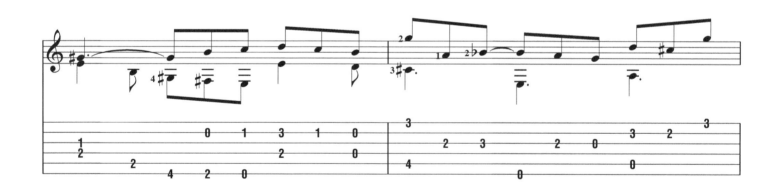

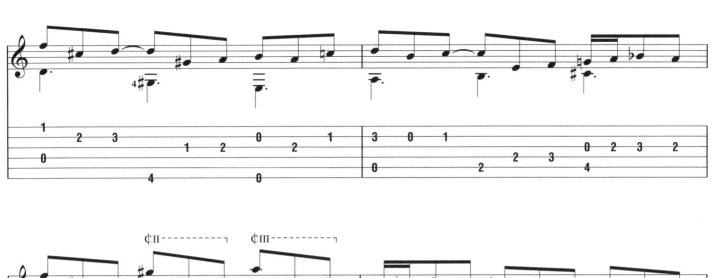

Aria - Cantata No. 39

Johann Sebastian Bach

Moderately

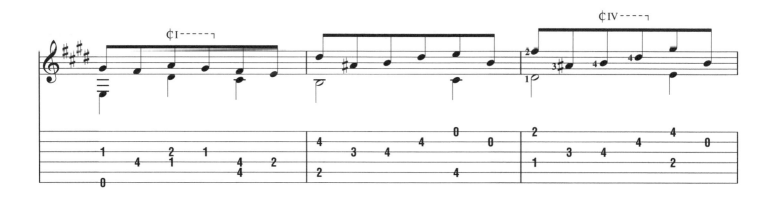

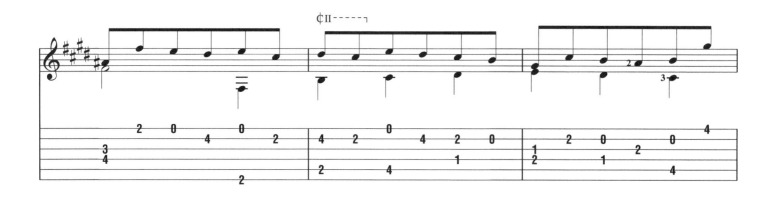

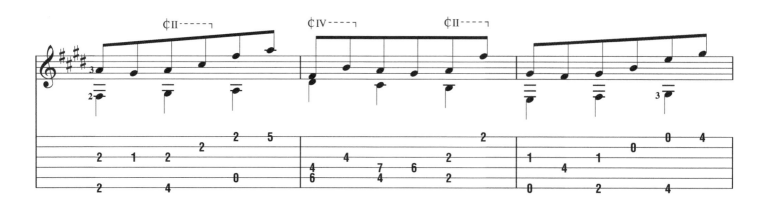

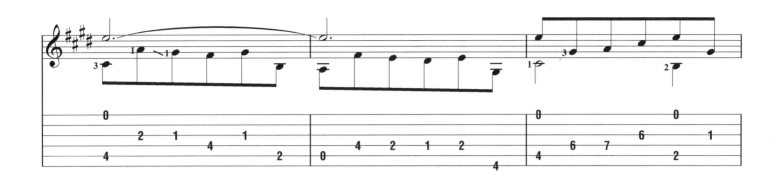

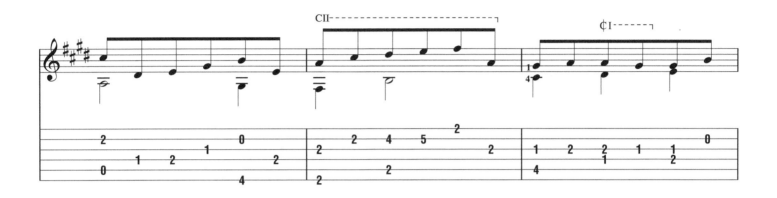

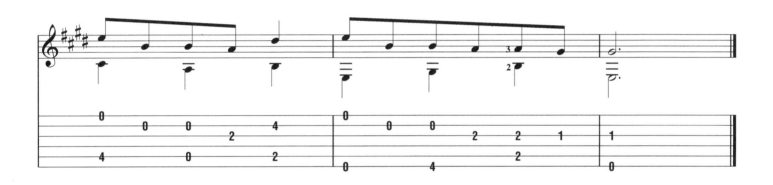

Aria - Cantata No. 57

TRACK 9

Johann Sebastian Bach

Moderately

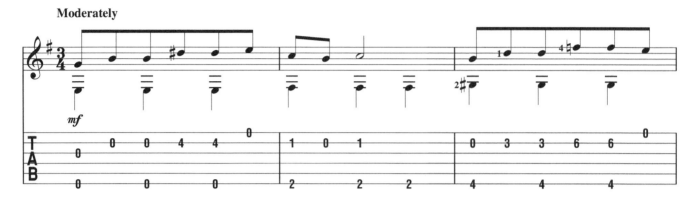

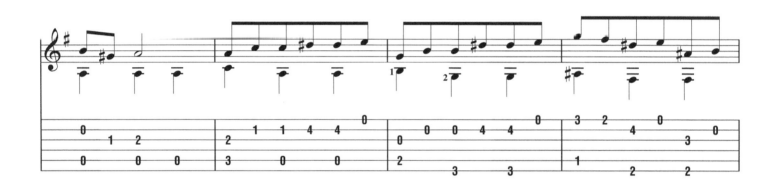

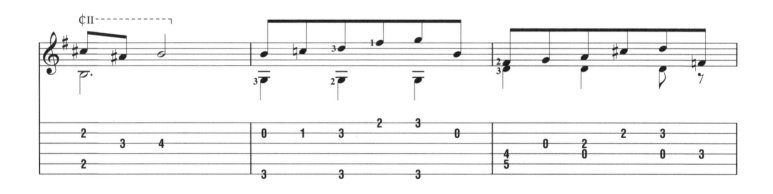

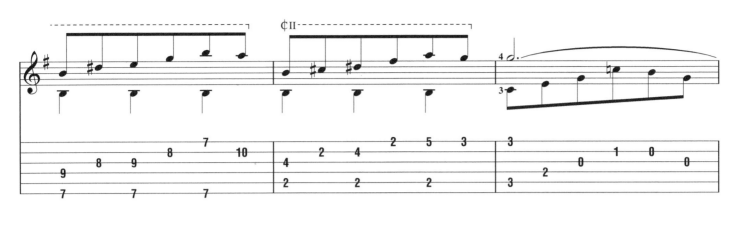

Aria - Cantata No. 77

Johann Sebastian Bach

Moderately bright

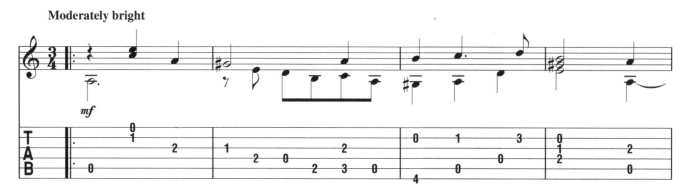

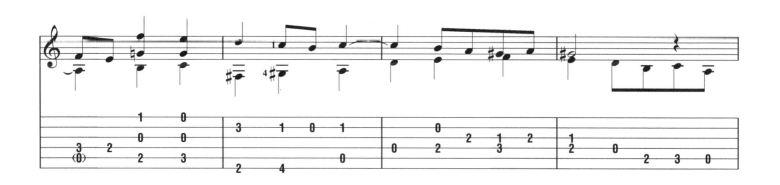

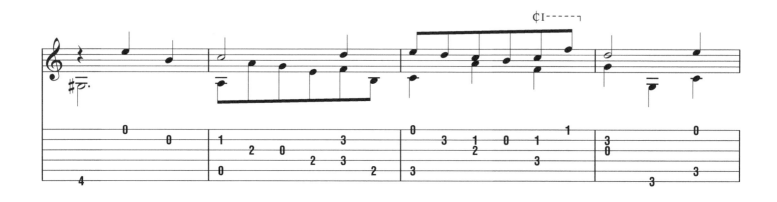

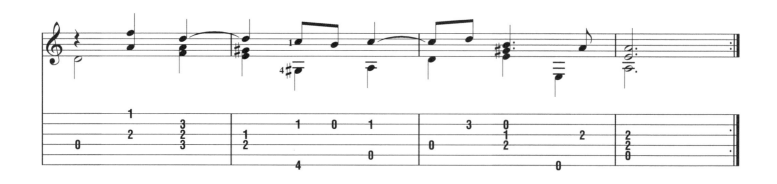

Aria - Cantata No. 98

TRACK 11

Johann Sebastian Bach

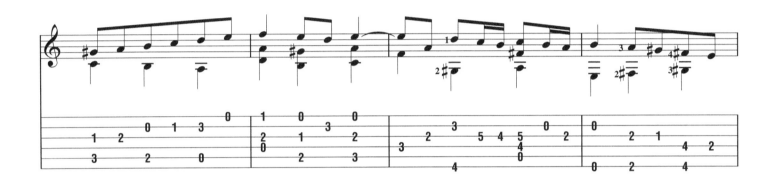

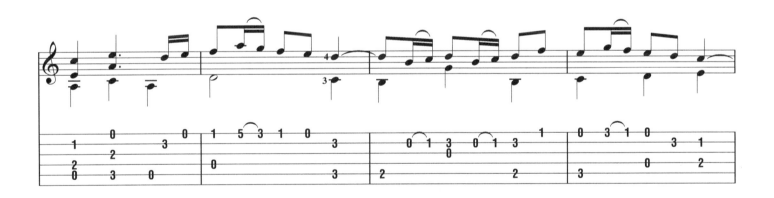

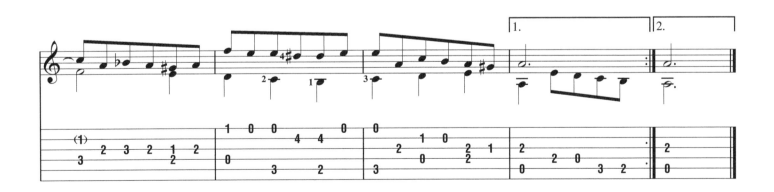

Aria - Cantata No. 79

TRACK 12

Johann Sebastian Bach

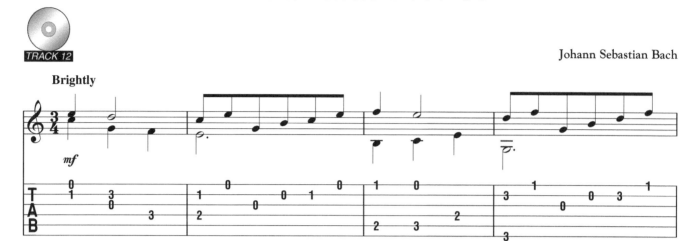

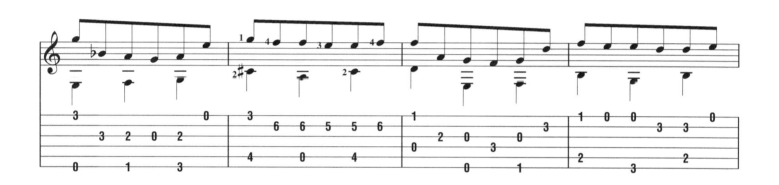

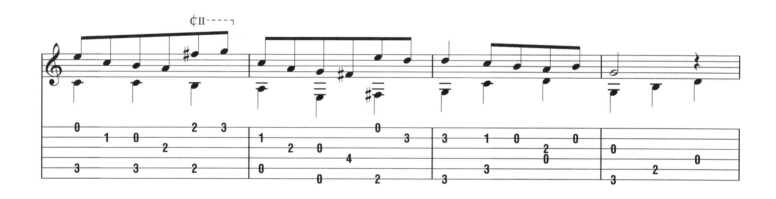

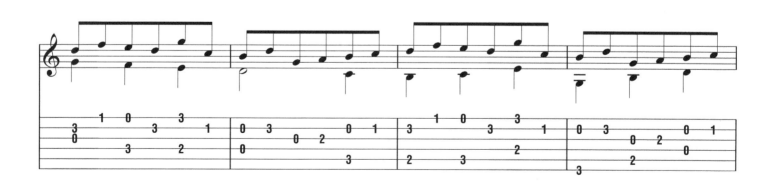

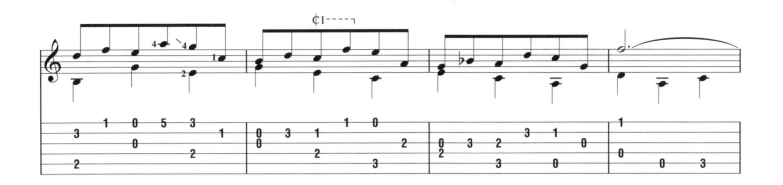

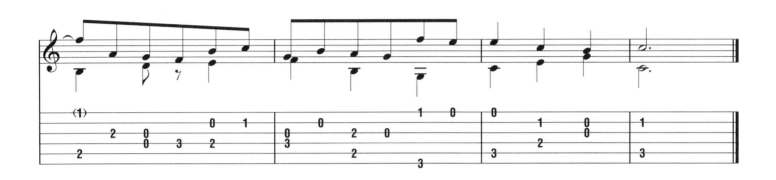

Aria - Cantata No. 85

TRACK 13

Johann Sebastian Bach

Moderately slow, in 2

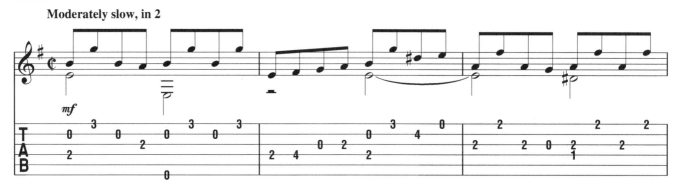

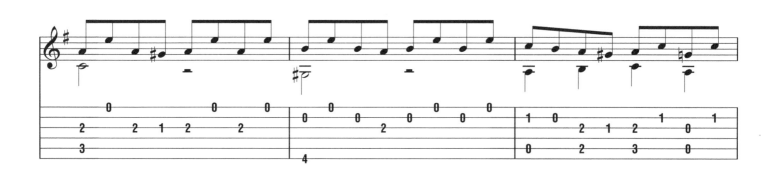

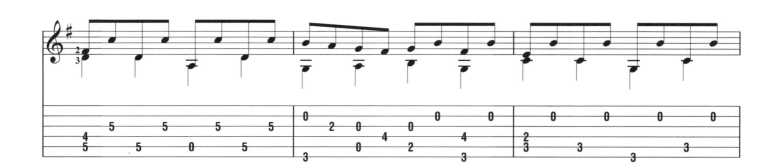

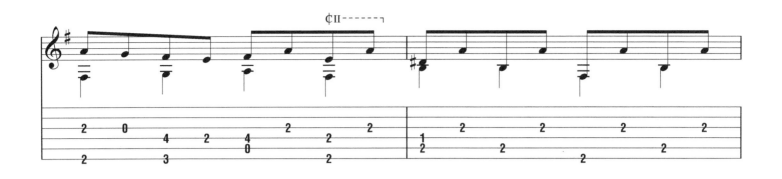

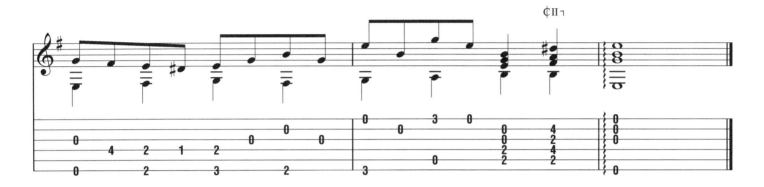

Aria - Cantata No. 115

TRACK 14

Johann Sebastian Bach

Slowly, in 2

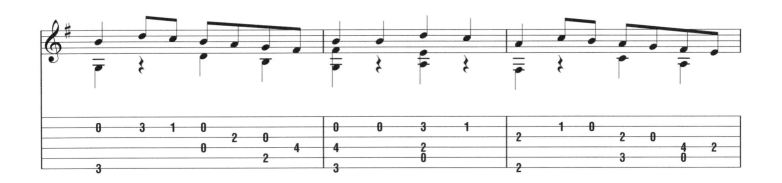

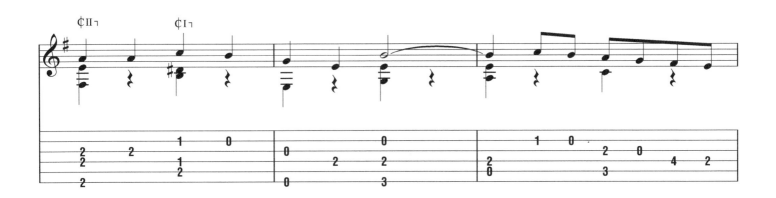

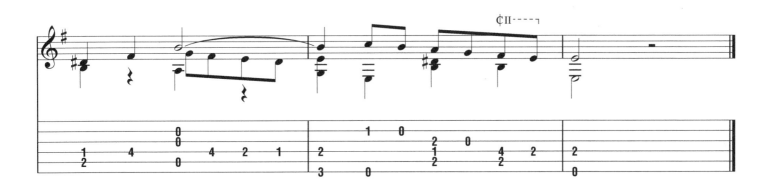

Aria - Cantata No. 116

Johann Sebastian Bach

TRACK 15

Moderately

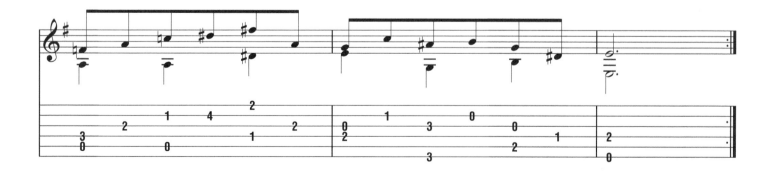

Aria - Cantata No. 140

TRACK 16

Johann Sebastian Bach

Moderately, in 2

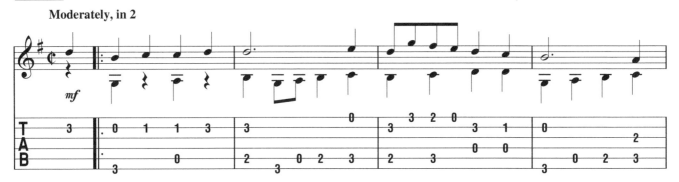

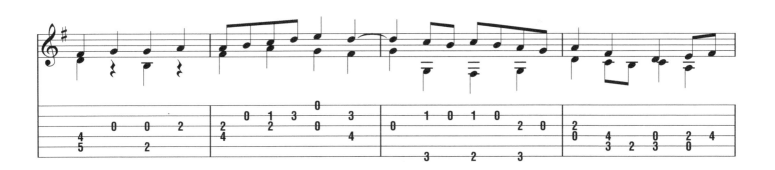

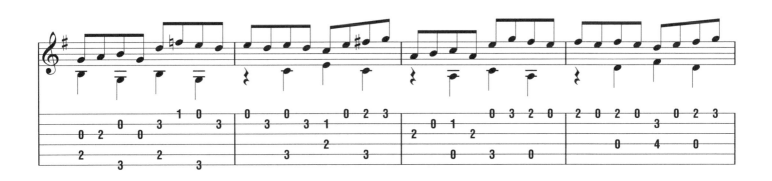

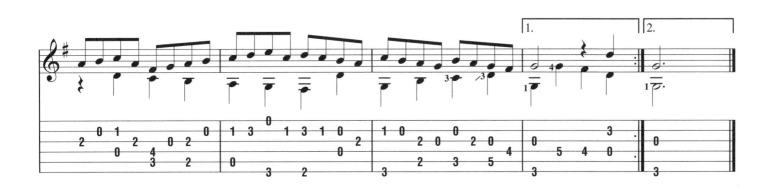

Aria - Cantata No. 119

TRACK 17

Johann Sebastian Bach

Slowly, in 1

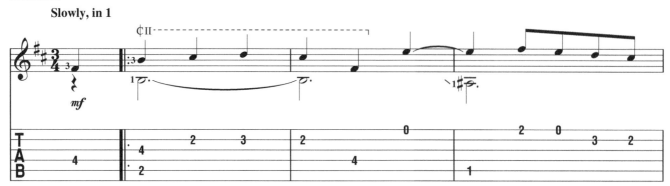

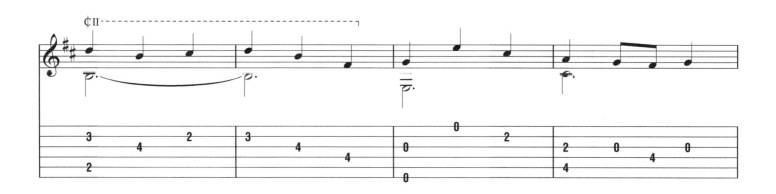

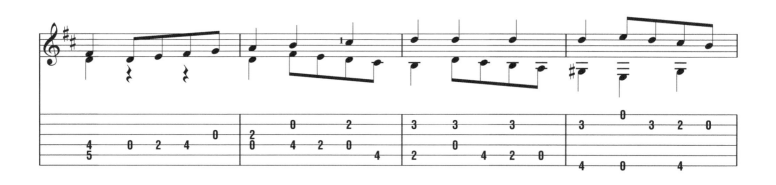

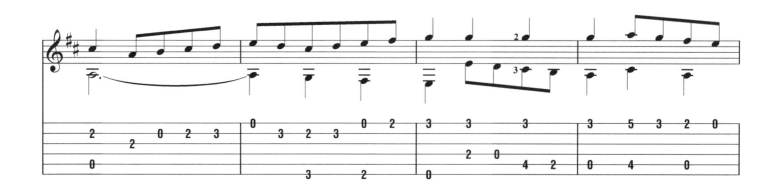

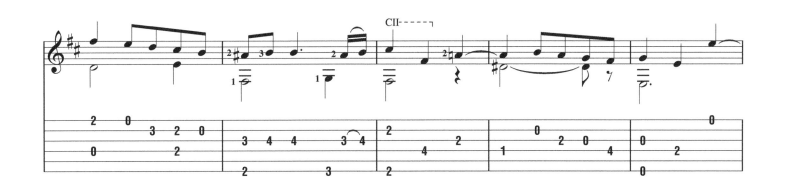

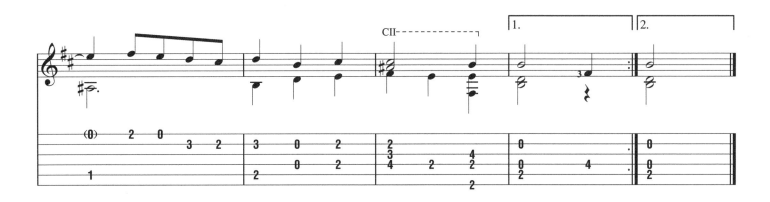

Aria - Cantata No. 152

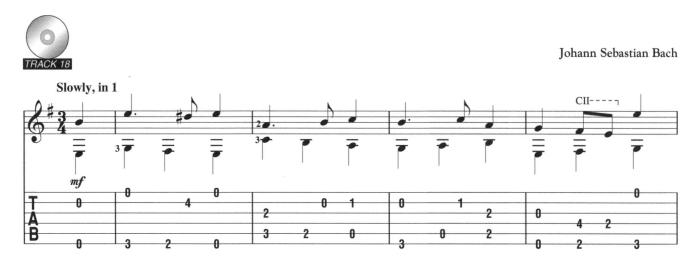

Johann Sebastian Bach

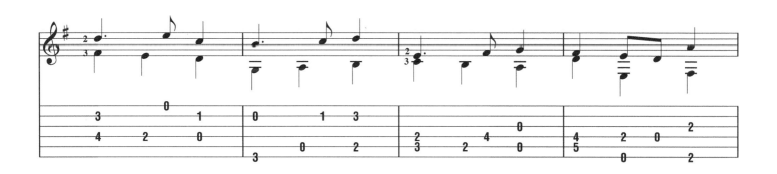

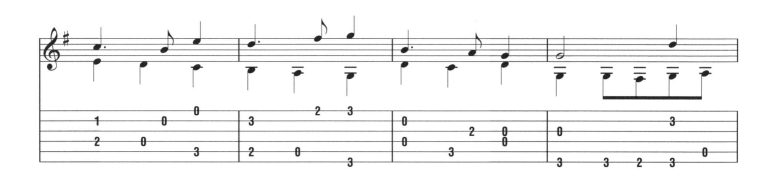

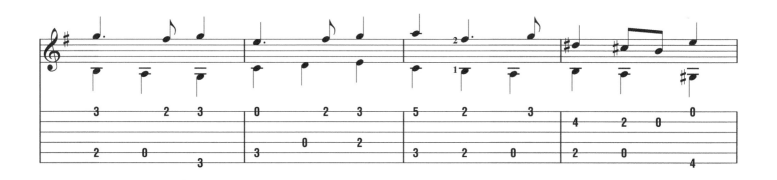

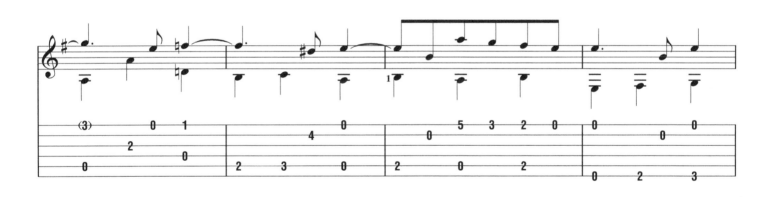

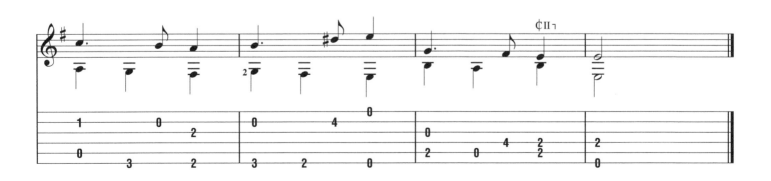

Aria - Cantata No. 170

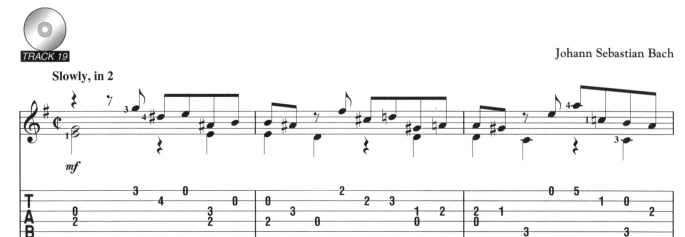

TRACK 19

Johann Sebastian Bach

Slowly, in 2

mf

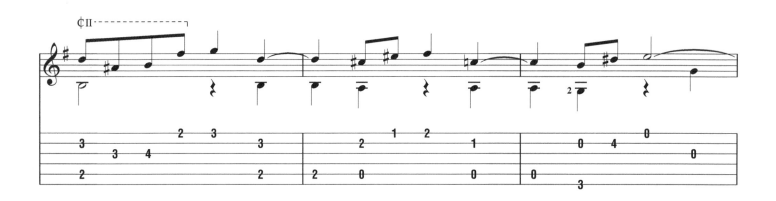

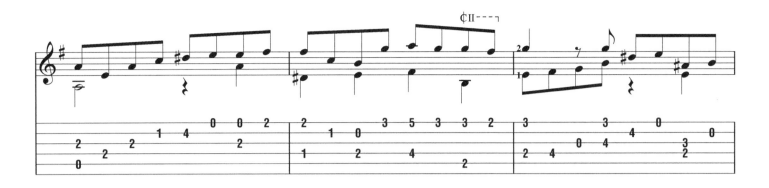

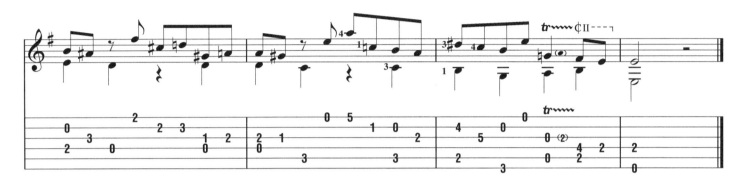

Aria - Cantata No. 186

TRACK 20

Johann Sebastian Bach

Slowly, in 1

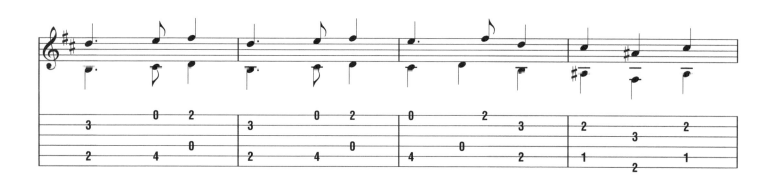

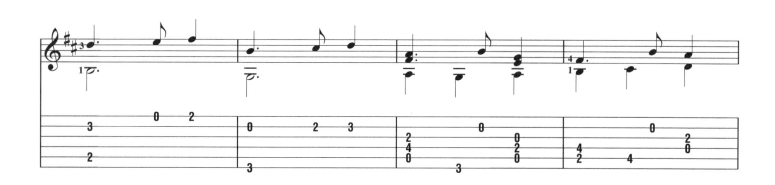

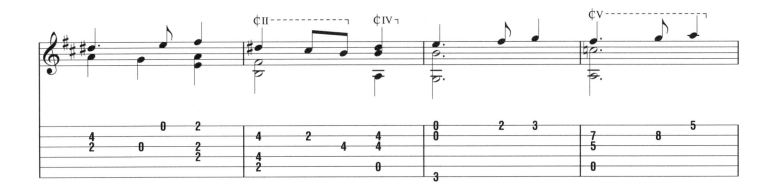

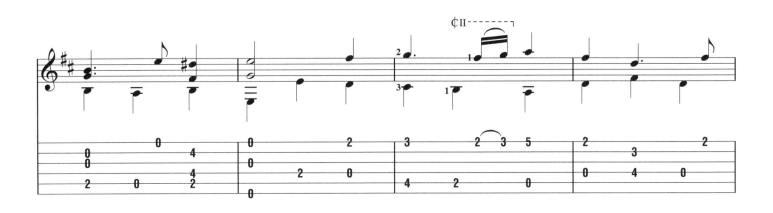

Aria - Easter Oratorio

TRACK 21

Johann Sebastian Bach

Slowly

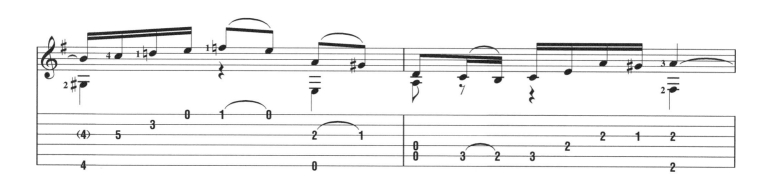

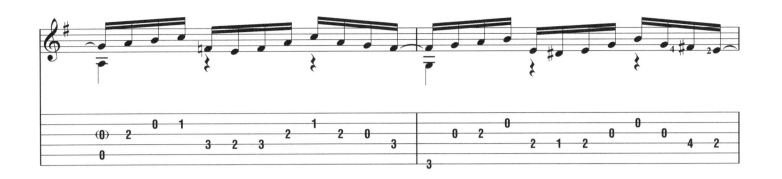

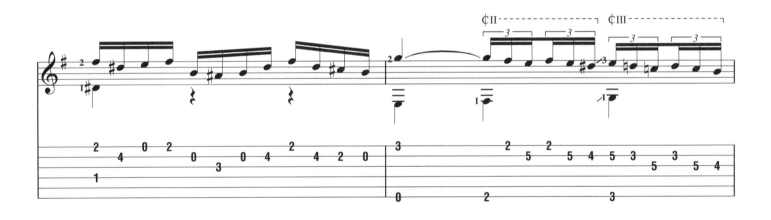

Aria - Saint John Passion

TRACK 22

Johann Sebastian Bach

Moderately

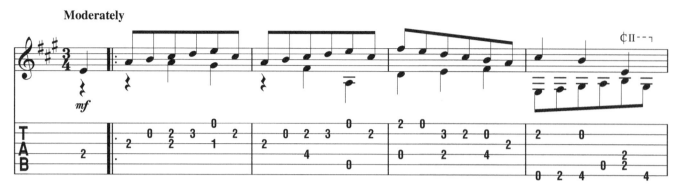

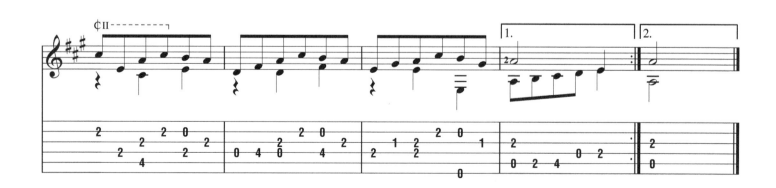

Air on the G String

Johann Sebastian Bach

TRACK 23

Moderately

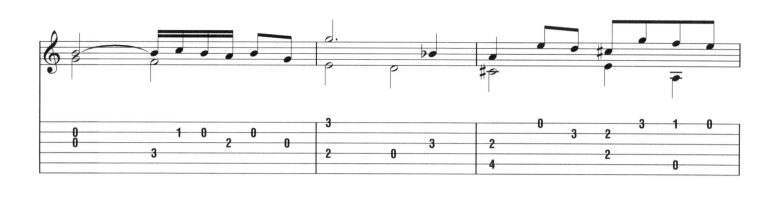

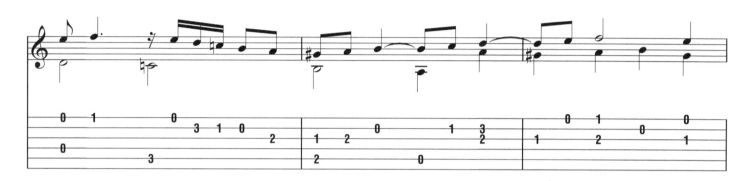

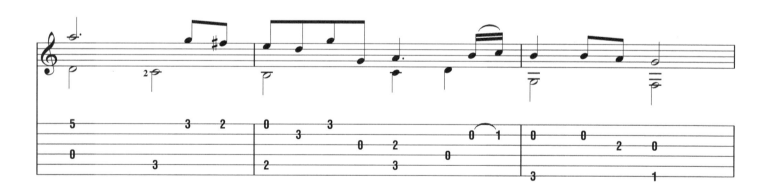

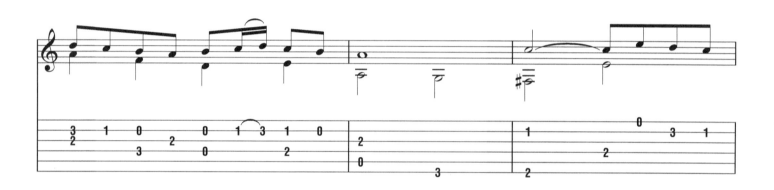

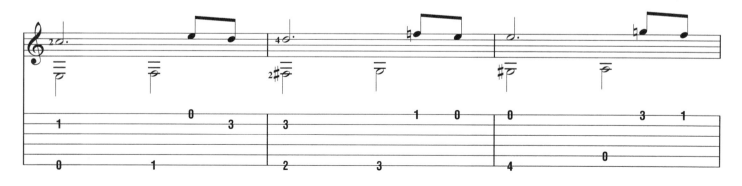

Air
(from the Notebook for Anna Magdelena)

Johann Sebastian Bach

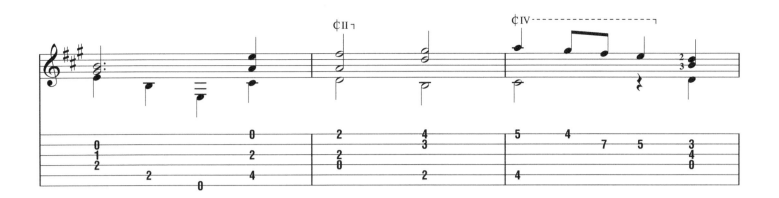

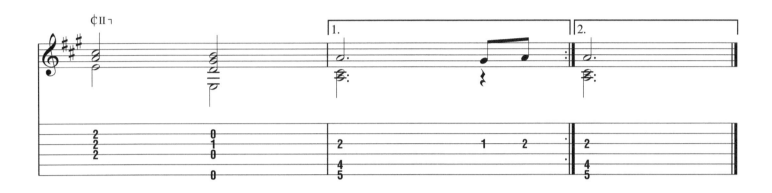

Arioso

TRACK 25

Johann Sebastian Bach

Moderately slow

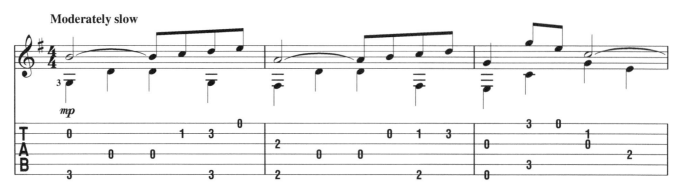

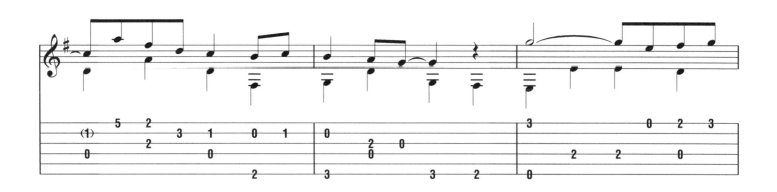

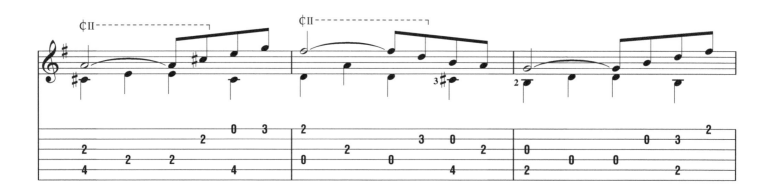

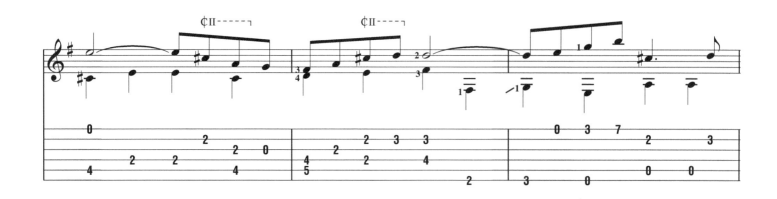

Be Thou with Me

TRACK 26

Johann Sebastian Bach

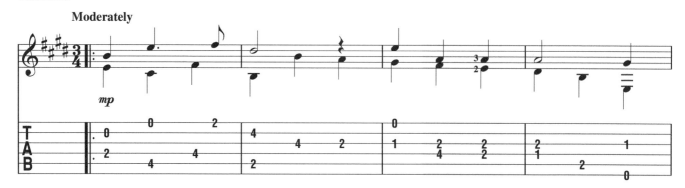

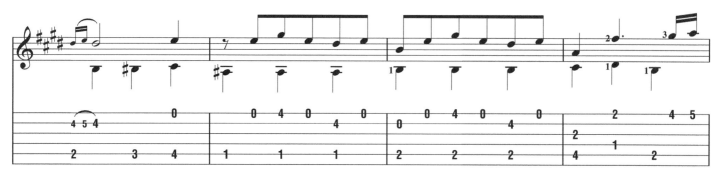

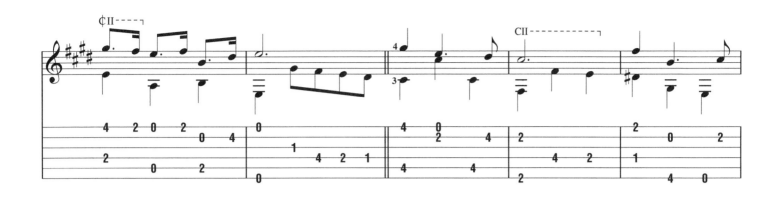

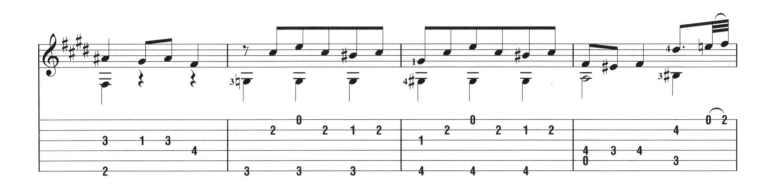

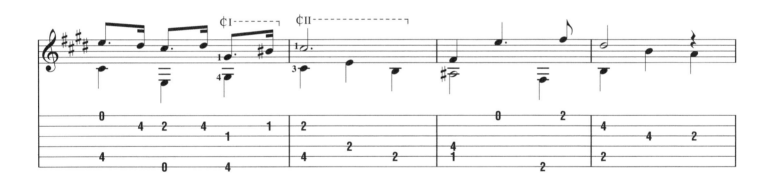

Bourrée

Johann Sebastian Bach

Moderately bright

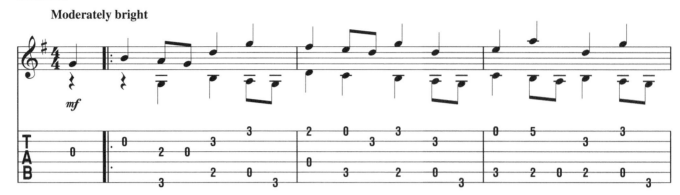

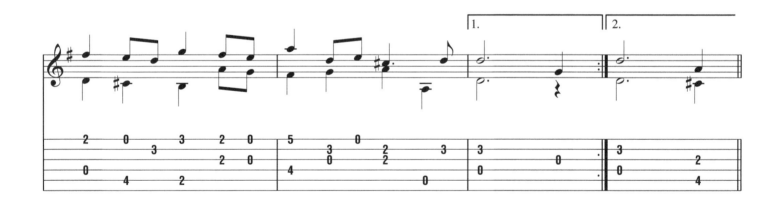

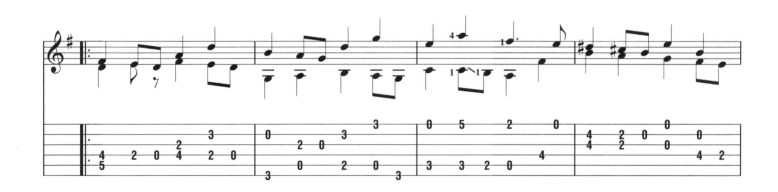

Bourrée
(from Cello Suite No. 3)

Johann Sebastian Bach

Moderately

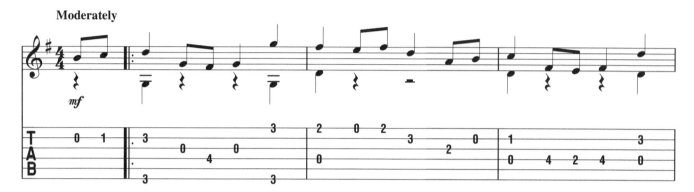

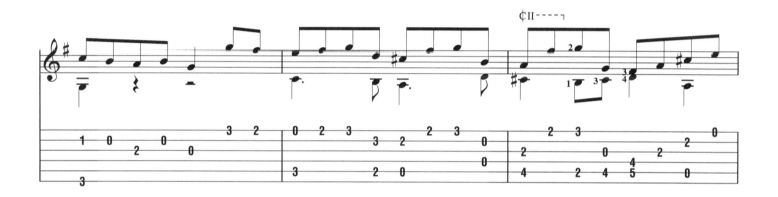

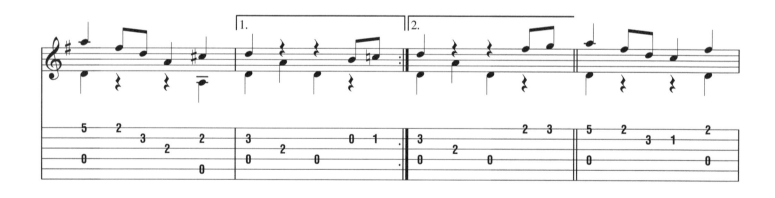

Bourrée
(from French Overture)

Johann Sebastian Bach

TRACK 29

Moderately bright

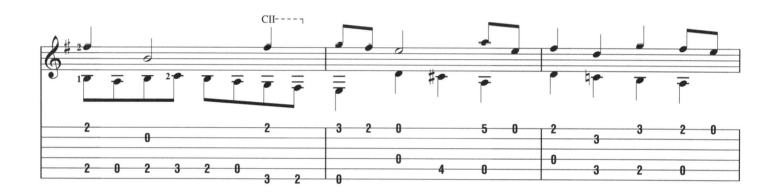

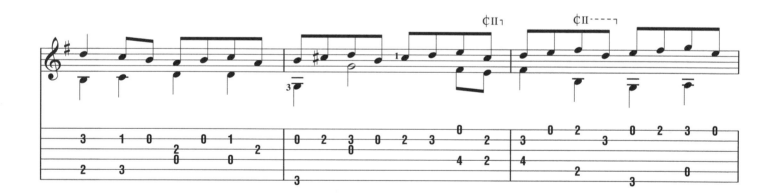

Bourrée
(from Violin Sonata No. 2)

Johann Sebastian Bach

TRACK 30

Moderately bright

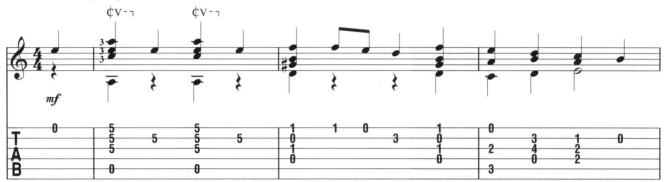

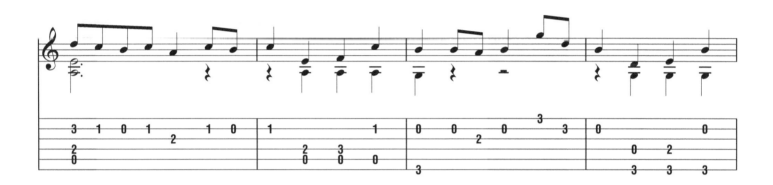

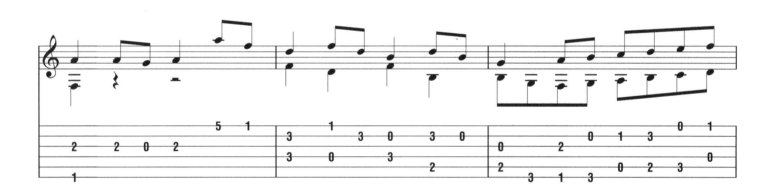

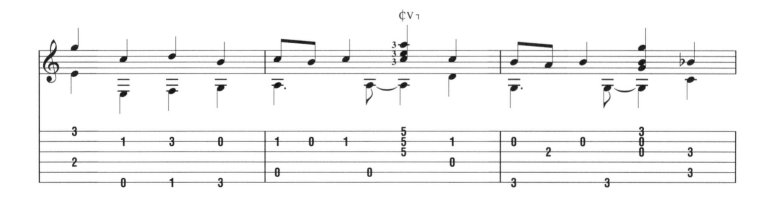

54

Bourrée in E Minor

Johann Sebastian Bach

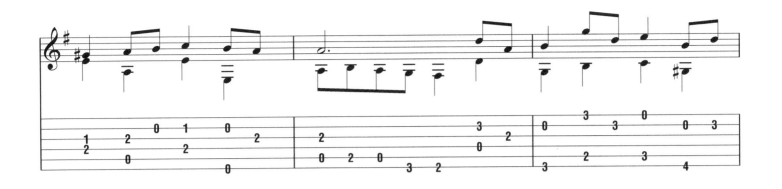

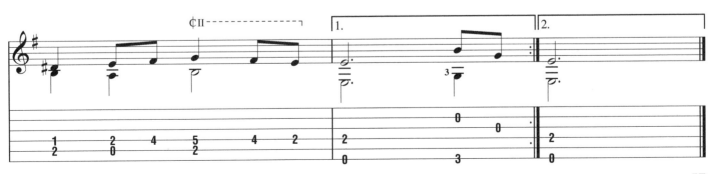

Chorale

(from Saint Matthew Passion)

Johann Sebastian Bach

TRACK 32

Moderately

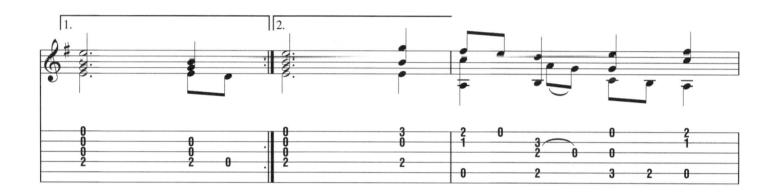

Come Again from Out the Dark Tomb

TRACK 33

Johann Sebastian Bach

Moderately

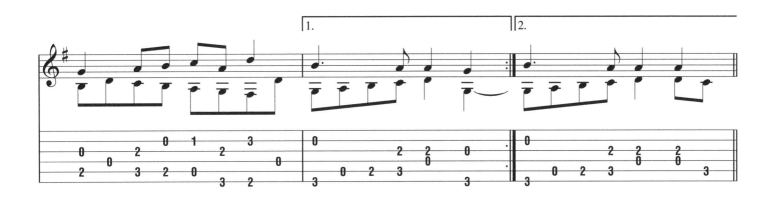

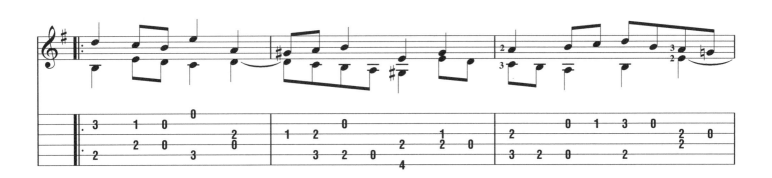

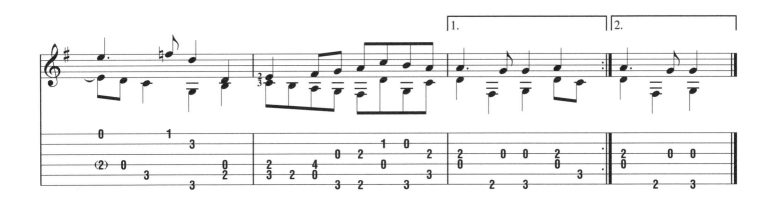

The Departure

(from The Journey)

Johann Sebastian Bach

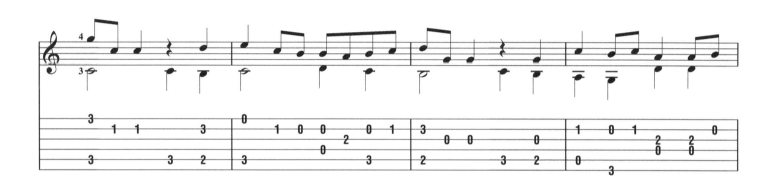

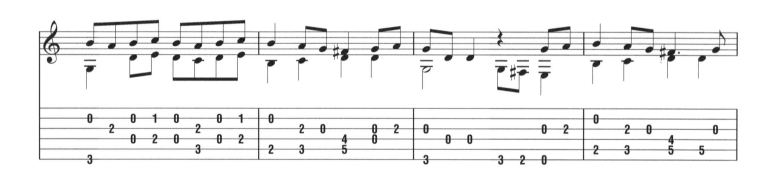

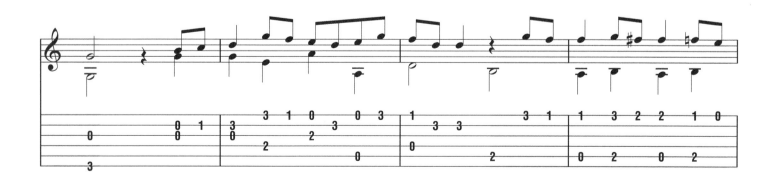

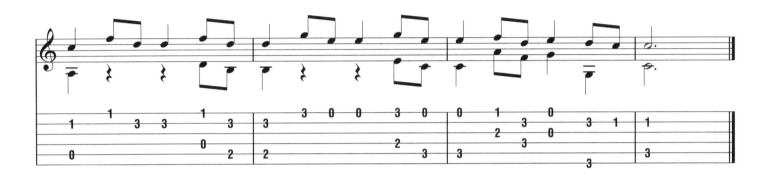

Gavotte
(from French Suite No. 5)

TRACK 35

Johann Sebastian Bach

Lively

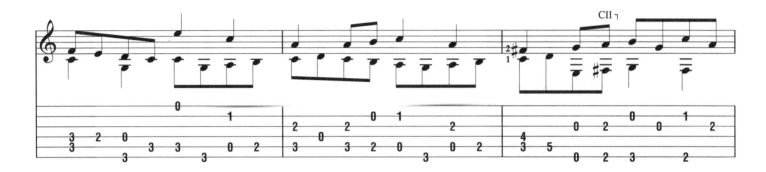

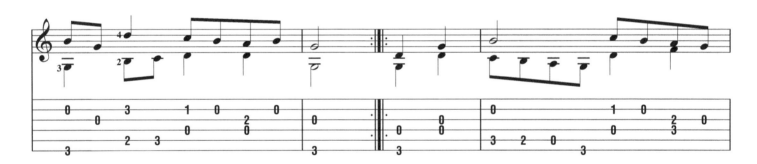

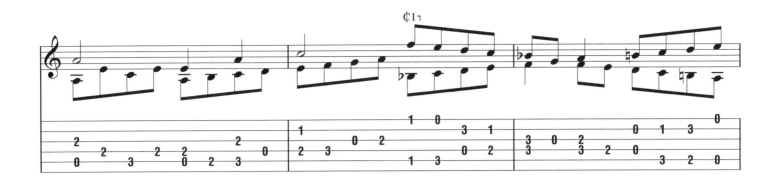

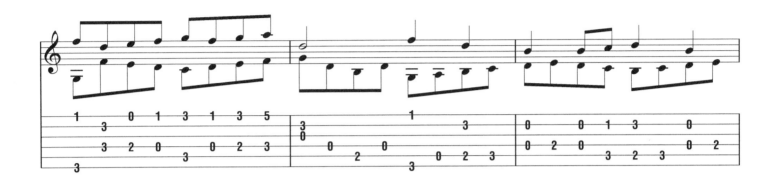

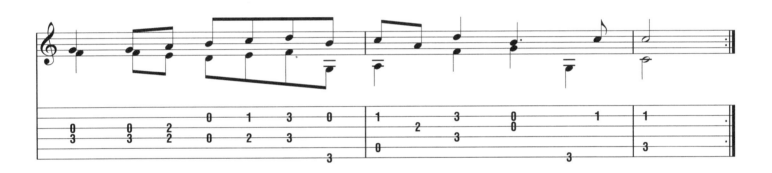

I Would Beside My Lord Be Watching

Johann Sebastian Bach

TRACK 36

Moderately slow, in 2

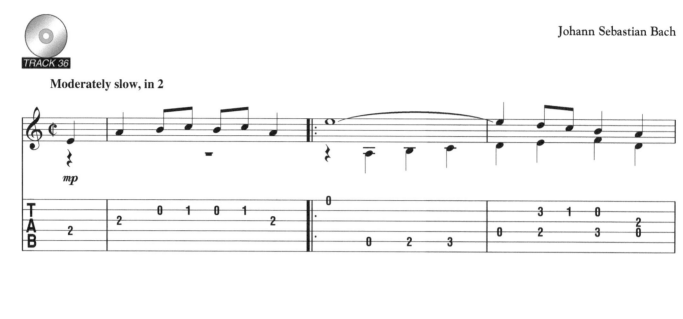

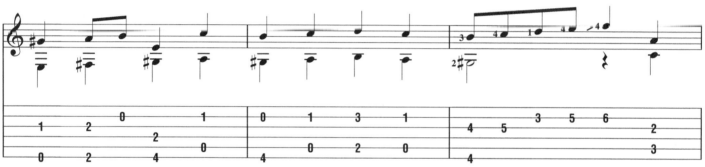

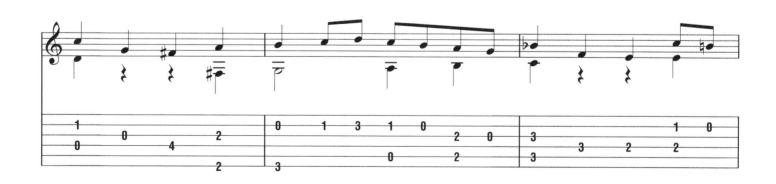

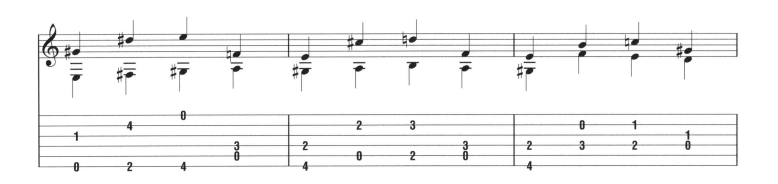

Jesu, Joy of Man's Desiring

TRACK 37

Johann Sebastian Bach

Tune 6th string to D

Moderately slow

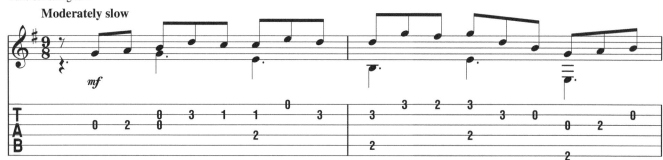

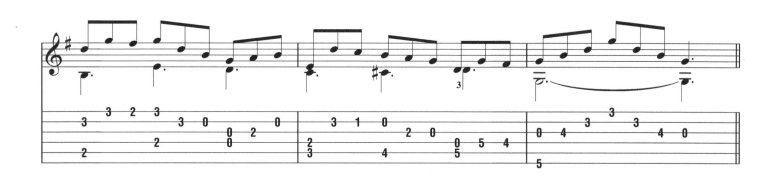

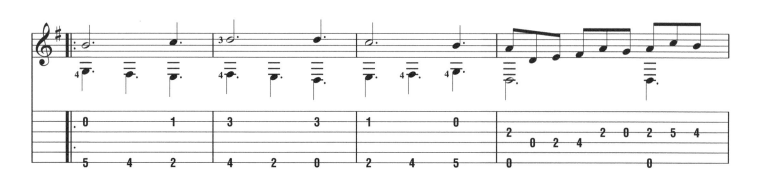

Jesu, My Joy

Johann Sebastian Bach

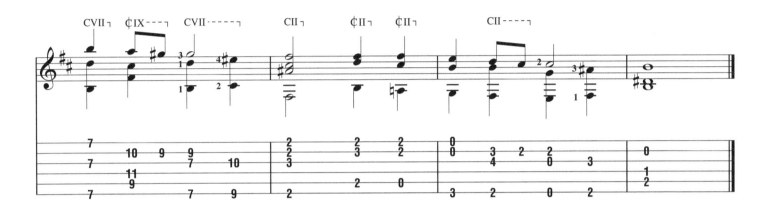

Minuet

(from French Suite No. 3)

Johann Sebastian Bach

⑥ = D

Moderately fast

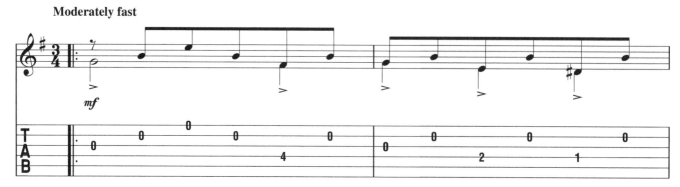

My Life Is Now Almost Gone

Johann Sebastian Bach

Minuet 1

(from the Notebook for Anna Magdelena)

Johann Sebastian Bach

Moderately

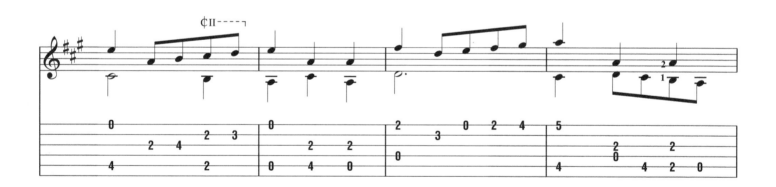

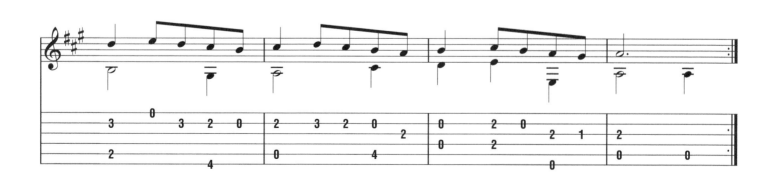

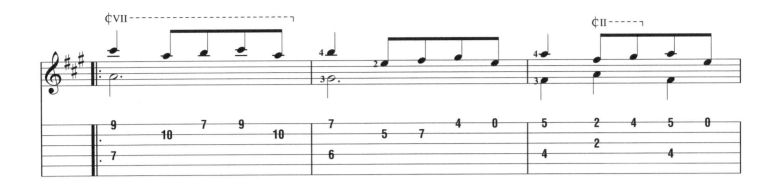

Minuet 2

(from the Notebook for Anna Magdelena)

Johann Sebastian Bach

Tune 6th string to D

Moderately

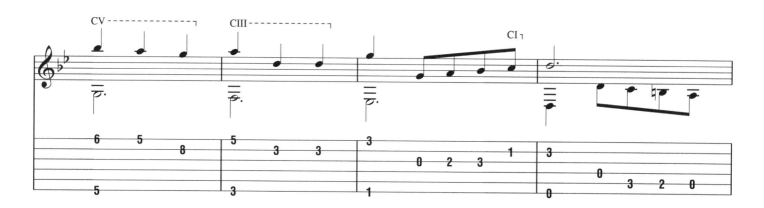

Minuet 3

(from the Notebook for Anna Magdelena)

Johann Sebastian Bach

Not So Sadly, Not So Deeply

Johann Sebastian Bach

O Gloomy Night, When Wilt Thou

Johann Sebastian Bach

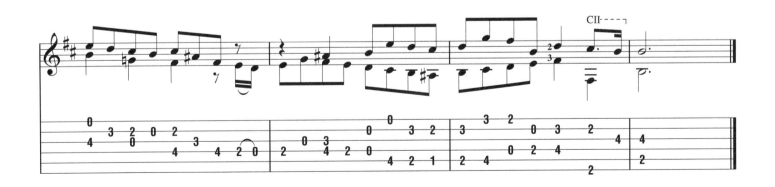

One Thing Is Needed, O Lord, This One Thing

Johann Sebastian Bach

TRACK 46

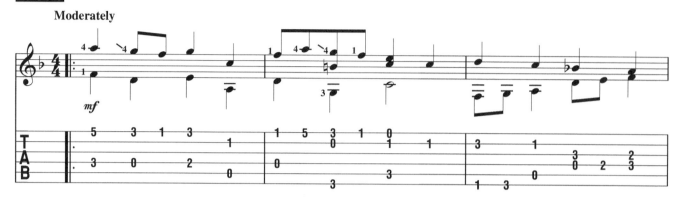

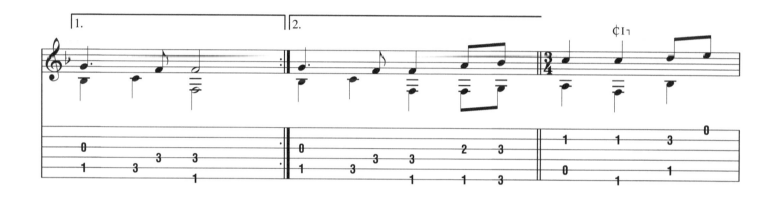

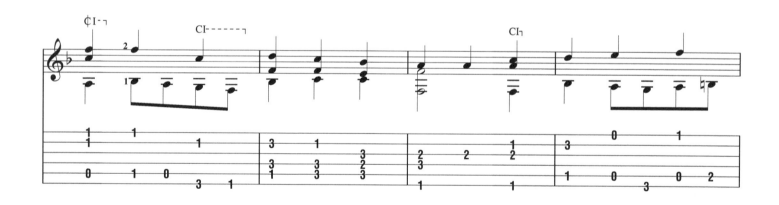

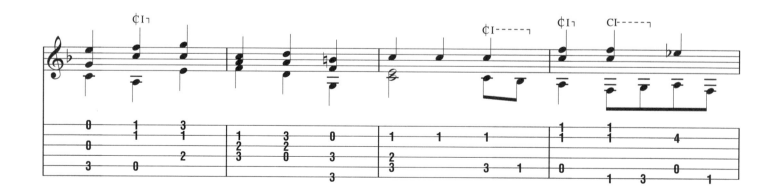

Sleepers, Wake

Johann Sebastian Bach

Moderately slow, in 2

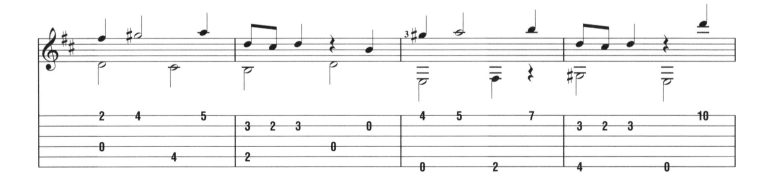

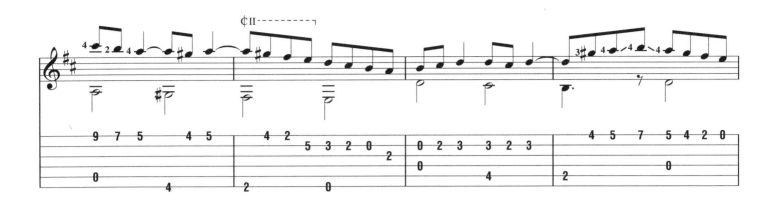

Sinfonia
(from Christmas Oratorio)

Johann Sebastian Bach

TRACK 48

Sorrow and Regret

(from *The Journey*)

Johann Sebastian Bach

Moderately slow

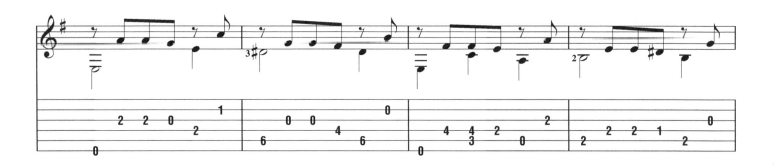

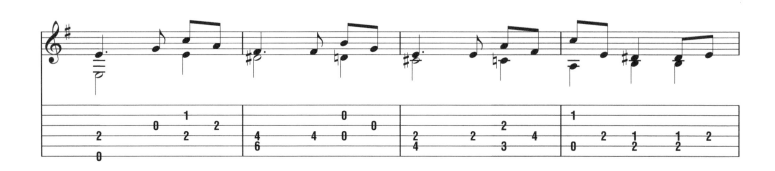

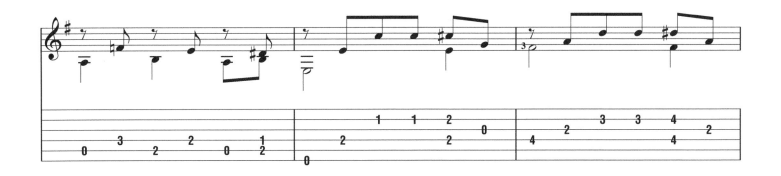

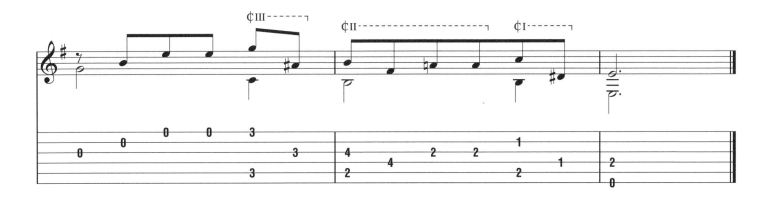

Sheep May Safely Graze

Johann Sebastian Bach

Moderately slow, in 2

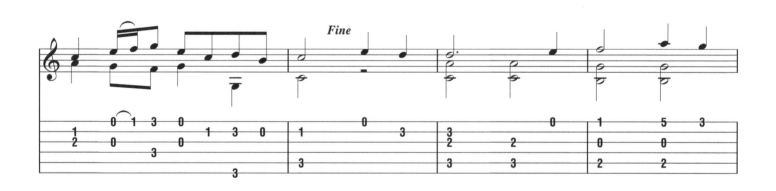